Coaching Questions

101 Coaching Questions for the Coach and the Coaching Client for an Empowering Coaching Session

by Randy Wayne

© **Copyright 2016 by Randy Wayne**
- All rights reserved.

This document is geared towards providing exact and reliable information in regards to the topic and issue covered. The publication is sold with the idea that the publisher is not required to render accounting, officially permitted, or otherwise, qualified services. If advice is necessary, legal or professional, a practiced individual in the profession should be ordered.

- From a Declaration of Principles which was accepted and approved equally by a Committee of the American Bar Association and a Committee of Publishers and Associations.

In no way is it legal to reproduce, duplicate, or transmit any part of this document in either electronic means or in printed format. Recording of this publication is strictly prohibited and any storage of this document is not allowed unless with written permission from the publisher. All rights reserved.

The information provided herein is stated to be truthful and consistent, in that any liability, in terms of inattention or otherwise, by any usage or abuse of any policies, processes, or directions contained within is the solitary and utter responsibility of the recipient reader. Under no circumstances will any legal responsibility or blame be held against the publisher for any reparation, damages, or monetary loss due to the information herein, either directly or indirectly.

Respective authors own all copyrights not held by the publisher.

The information herein is offered for informational purposes solely, and is universal as so. The presentation of the information is without contract or any type of guarantee assurance.

The trademarks that are used are without any consent, and the publication of the trademark is without permission or backing by the trademark owner. All trademarks and brands within this book are for clarifying purposes only and are the owned by the owners themselves, not affiliated with this document.

Disclaimer

Some of the links in this book may be affiliate links. If you click on them and decide to buy something, I may or may not get paid a commission. This doesn't mean that it will cost you extra money. I only include links to products or services that I think are valuable or I use myself.

TABLE OF CONTENTS

INTRODUCTION 6

CHAPTER 1: What is coaching 8

CHAPTER 2: Why a Session Needs Specific Questions 11

CHAPTER 3: Types of Coaching 14

CHAPTER 4: Media to Help with Coaching 20

CHAPTER 5: Questions for a Coach to Ask 22

CHAPTER 6: Questions for a Person to Know 38

CHAPTER 7: Client Coaching Questions to Ask 49

CHAPTER 8: Questions for the Client to Ask Themselves ... 58

CONCLUSION 68

INTRODUCTION

Hello and thank you for taking the time to check out this book!

For many of us, the concept of coaching and life coaching might be something we are not used to. All too often, there are times when we as people assume that we understand how something works, when in truth it is not always that way. However, the element of coaching can help you understand what you need to know about this, and over time, you will be able to really get what you need with this, and sometimes, it makes a coaching session that much better.

With many people, they often want to find the answers themselves, but in truth, it can be hard. With coaching, for many people, they do need that other person, or sometimes they just need to be pushed into the right direction. Coaching will allow you to do just that, and so much more as well.

In this book, you will learn all about the nuances of coaching. This means that you will learn not only what coaching is about, but also some of the various facets and different elements of this, and how you as well can be a better coach. There are even questions for a coach or client o ask themselves, and you will learn why you ask that, and even the best possible answers for that sort of thing. Give yourself the coaching that you deserve, and you will be able to definitely and for sure have an all-around good coaching session. We will go over types of coaching as well, because there are different elements to coaching that can be a bit different for you, and this can be seen in many different ways. On the other hand, with coaching, you will be able to take whatever issues you have at hand and work on them. This book will guide you in the right direction, and by the end of this, you will know exactly how to be the best coach you can be, and the best client to a coach as well.

CHAPTER 1:
What is coaching

Now, your first question might be what coaching is. Coaching is an exact form of betterment, and often, people do not realize just what it can pertain to. This chapter however, will go over just what coaching is, and how it can relate to your life.

Now, coaching is basically like what it is, it is someone that you have that is working with another person to help the other person's goal. Fr example, think of coaches in sports teams. Many times, you have that person who is on the side cheering you on, telling you how to do the action without royally screwing everything up. That in essence, is coaching. In truth, it can be something that people can get into to help them, and it is definitely a way to improve the relationships between two people.

Sometimes this is done in a very formal setting, where you actually go to an office, and the two of you converse there. In other cases, it is an informal setting, where there is a relationship between two people, and the two of you occasionally meet up, and in truth, it is obvious that there are both formal and informal elements to this. For some people, the coach might be someone who has more experience, or who even has expert knowledge on a subject to give advice to the other person. The client in that case would be the one receiving the advice, and using that to better a goal. In truth, coaching works o have different tasks at hand along with some objectives, along with some good development goals and general goals as well. Sometimes, you can even coach each other if the two of you are working to both overcome one sort of problem. It can be used if you have a goal that needs to be overcome, or if there is a problem you need to face.

Often, there is professional coaching that one can do. It can involve anything including improving communication skills, getting a different perspective on various elements, or even questioning or contradicting your original idea to see things from a different angle. Often, you can use this is all types of coaching, and you can use this to help overcome some sort of behavior, whether it be one that is a health problem, a personal problem, a social issue, some spiritual problem, or any sort of element. Coaching is there to help the person overcome the odds and beat it.

For some, coaching might seem like a silly thing. Some of us like to fly solo, but often, we need the help we can get from this. We might need that extra little boost, and it can be used not only to help businesses and people grow, but it can even help with mental issues such as ADHD and other much problems. Spiritual coaching can be used to help with mental issues too, and it is a means to really get you in the right sort of frame of min to look at a problem differently.

With coaching, you will be able to think critically and outside the box as well. Often, when we're going through business and personal transactions, we do not look at anything past the personal level. We only look at that, and we might look at the various elements of that too. But, let's look at it from another way, and often, big problems can be fixed in that regard. For some, it can do a whole lot of good, and in others, it can be something that can make a difference in their life in various ways.

Doing something about a problem can help a lot, and with coaching, you will be able to tackle the problem terminated, and work out a good, adequate solution to achieve the success you deserve. With coaching, you will be able to do just that, and so much more in various ways. Coaching has a lot of various elements to it that can help you, and it is something that everyone should get into.

CHAPTER 2:
Why a Session Needs Specific Questions

Now, when you are coaching, sometimes you might wonder why you need specific questions. Specific questions are something that can help another person really think outside the box and work towards success in areas of life. For many people, being specific is the difference between a successful and some unsuccessful coaching. This chapter will go over what specific questions are, and what role they are striving to play in terms of where to go with this.

What are Specific Questions?

In a coaching session, you get asked various questions all of different types and mentions. For some people, it might be little questions about life and the state of it, and for others, it might be geared towards a specific action. With questions, you will be able to prompt a good response out of the client, and from there, you will have much more success.

Let's take a coaching session where you do not really ask specific questions. Maybe you just ask general ones like "what do you want to do?" or something of that nature. Yes, that is a good one once you have the problem figured out, but it is not where you should go with this. Specific questions are there to direct not only the client, but the coach as well.

If you do not tackle the specific problem at hand, you will not be successful in fixing it and bringing it back to a better state. Let's face it, a lot of us do refuse to face our problems, and many times, we just do not realize it until it is too late. Then again, with specific questions, you as a coach will be able to tackle the issue at hand, and you will be able to go over with the client exactly what is going wrong. Often, a problem with coaching is not necessarily the fact that you are coaching; it is the wrong types of questions. In a coaching session, it does make a difference whether you guide the person, or if you do not guide them. If they just go around willy-nilly, chances are, they will avoid what's really going on, and instead, they will suffer from there.

That's why you have specific questions. These questions will directly relate to what is afflicting the person at hand. This can be anything from financial issues, to even issues in their personal life such as marriage and the like. You as a coach need to direct the person's attention, allowing them to face the problem, and make the decision. These questions are used in that way, and the more specific you are, the more chances you will be able to handle the problem at hand as well.

For the Client

Now, these specific questions do not just benefit the coach, but they do the client as well. It is pretty important to see what the client can do to benefit from this, for there is a lot of elements this has to offer, and for a client, this can make quite the difference.

For starters, your client is definitely floating about, needing help and unable to do anything about it. That's what it is like. Often, if they need help figuring out a solution, chances are they've tried other things, and in general, they cannot do a damn thing about it. It sucks, but that is the way that it is with some of these people. For many of them, they might not realize just what they have to do until it is too late. But with coaching, it will take their attention and direct it accordingly.

A general question wont' help them face the problem. It just will not, and that's the truth of the matter. In this sort of situation, you need to be specific, honest, and you need to look at it from the right angles. Instead of always looking at it in a general sense, you can get specific and from there, start to work on improving your life with this in mind. With specific questions, you will be able to take exactly what you have learned and use it in a more concrete manner.

With general questions, they do work well to get the mind going. As a coach or client, they are very important to have, especially if the client and coach aren't really on good terms as of yet. But in truth, you do need to have those specific questions on hand to help you improve your life, because often, it can make a huge difference between being open about various parts of life, and not being open. When you are trying to coach, you want the client to be open and willing to speak, and often, that is done via questions that aren't always super general, but instead really nitpick at the brain, get the person to dive into their psyche, and from there, improve their life and the way that it works.

This book will go over 101 questions to help with a coaching session, and many of these will specifically get the person on the right track to help them solidify and improve the relationship they have with the subject, and along with that, you will be able to have much more success at the end of the day as well. Be smart, work on your coaching sessions and questions, and from there, you will do even better than you ever thought possible.

CHAPTER 3:
Types of Coaching

With coaching, there are many different types. It is not just used for a businessperson or the like, but it can also tackle specific problems as well. This chapter will go over just what types of coaching there are, and even some tidbits about this sort of coaching, and why it might be in your best interests to try these out.

Spiritual coaching

With this sort of coaching, it can relate to Christianity in the sense that it does involve sometimes using tenets from that religion, and sometimes it can be a practitioner of that relation. Yet, it is not generally the situation, and regularly, with this type of coaching, it can be used to improve the connection one has spiritually with that of the material world.

Often, for many who practice religion and spirituality, they struggle to tap into that. That's where this coaching comes in. it swoops in so you can take the spiritual nature of yourself, or even of a heavenly body such as god, and from there, use the various elements of this to improve your lot. It is helpful, especially for those who have a bit of a religious sense to them and know for sure that this is exactly what they wanted.

Success coaching

Everyone wants success. It is obvious when people do. But sometimes, people need help working to getting success and being able to prosper, and this coaching helps with that.

With success coaching, it will go over just how to be successful in a different sort of manner, but not only that, it is also working out the kinks in life that are preventing you from being successful. Maybe there are personal blocks in the way, such as former friends who are now estranged but those words they had for you still resonate within. Whatever it may be, it is important that you make sure that you do realize there are various stops to the success of your life, and this type of coaching will work to help eliminate that sort of thing. With this sort of coaching, you can be a successful person in various fronts and manners, and you do not have to do much, besides follow the advice and work to implement it into your life. It is a good way to help work to improve your life, and give yourself the success you know you deserve.

Financial coaching

Another major problem with people is money. Money can be hard to manage, and often, people do not realize that they are bad with money until it is far too late. But often, there are means to fix this sort of problem, different sorts of actions you can take as a problem to improve your ability to handle money and be successful with it. That's where this type of coaching comes in.

Through financial coaching, you can obtain more information on how to handle money, different sorts of actions you need to take to improve your ability to be smart with money. Money is not an easy to thing to cope with, and for some people, it can be quite the struggle. But do not let it get you down, instead let finical coaching take the reins, and from there, you will be able to improve your ability to not only have money, but to manage money as well.

Typically, this sort of coaching is done by someone who is versed in the realm of money and knowing how to deal with the dealings of it. It is a resource for those who are terrible with money, which needs an extra boost to have a good sort of experience with that sort of thing.

Fitness coaching

Now, this is coaching for the body, but it is not just someone who is there behind the guy at the gym as he or she does bench presses. Rather, it is also a sort of lifestyle coaching, used to help build a better life for the person, and to help improve the effectiveness of it.

For fitness coaching, it will go over what sort of parts of the body you want to fix up. This could be anything from losing a few pounds, to even making sure that you get the right sort of foods in your body to help you tone up. This type of coaching will also give you a plan of sorts to help you reach your goal. This can also fit under sports coaching as well, and it can be used to help those who are struggling with getting better at a sport, and from there, it can help to make it easier on everyone. This type of coaching is regulated towards the body, and that's what you will be working on, but as well, it might go over the mental barriers needed to help you lose weight, and from there, you can work to have a happier, healthier body in various sorts of ways, as well as having a better life for you and your peers a well.

Law of attraction coaching

The law of attraction is something that many people do refuse to look at initially, but it is a major part of being successful. Simply put, the law of attraction is a theory where you get what you attract, and you attract whatever it is that you do get based upon what sort of person and what sort of knowledge that you have. With that being said, essentially it is you get what you deserve, and often, this is what attributes to businesses being the law of attraction does work both ways, and for those that are working to improve their business, but just cannot seem to get it right, then this type of coaching is one that can be used unsuccessfully in various elements, and it can really make a difference for many people. With the law of attraction, you go over in detail what it is that you are doing that is causing issues, and from there, you can work the kinks out and do what you like. The law of attraction is a great way to work out stops in a business if you have tried everything else, and from there, you can implement other strategies and such that will work great for you.

Relationship coaching

Now on a more personal level are relationships. Relationships can either be easy, or they can be hard to manage. Some go well, others not so much. You might have a relationship with a family member or significant others, or even in a business or peer sense. Sometimes you might have a friend that you need to work something out with. Whatever it may be, often, you need to make sure that you are being smart about the decisions you make with this relationship. For many people, relationships can be hard once you start to see the issues at hand and you are working to cope with that. Nevertheless, with relationship coaching, you will be able to tackle the problem and terminated handle it.

This can work for future commitments in terms of a relationship as well. For marriages, this does work, because sometimes there are marital issues that need to be figured out before the couple can successfully move on with their life. There are also issues such as divorces that can require some sort of assistance with it. It is something that is often required to have some sort of solace and work with, but for many, it can be quite hard. However, with relationship coaching, you can take all of the coaching and apply it to your relationship issues, and from there, you can have much more success with it as well.

Business coaching

Business coaching is a way to help get businesses on the right track. It is typically used to develop human resources and strengthen a business. It will give those in the company the support that they need, feedback on actions, and it also gives advice to both individuals and groups to give a better sort of effectiveness in the business arena. Often, it is used to help get the clients on the way towards specific goals in the professional feels. For example, if you are looking to transfer to a new career, improve your performance, help with the organization and the effectiveness, and eve improving the executive presence, this is definitely the way that it changes it. It is also used to help with those that are struggling with the comfort of the organization, and from this, it is used to build a team that works to improve the performance in the workplace and along with that, create a sort of positive impact and improve the performance. It is a way to just improve businesses to make them better for everyone.

With coaching, there are many different outlets, various reasons to help you with this sort of thing. However, you will be able to take all of this and use it to your advantage, and from there, you will be able to work to improve all facets of life. With coaching, everything does get easier, but you will need to know exactly how to do it first, and what sorts of coaching questions you will need. Do not be afraid to dive into this, and do not worry about what might happen, for it is simple, yet effective, to know exactly where you want to go with this.

CHAPTER 4:
Media to Help with Coaching

Now, with coaching, there are various media that can be used to assist with the problems you might face. There are a lot of elements going around, and often, there are different sorts of issues at hand that can start to become pretty intricate over time. However, this chapter will go over the exact media necessary to improve your ability to have a better coaching session, and how to coach it adequately.

Calls

Some coaching can be as simple as calling on the phone. Talking on the phone is not only a great way to get over the fear of phone conversations, but also, to get over the nerves that seemed to become a bit stronger with those that talk. With phones, you will be able to really make it work out, and from there, you will be able to have much more success. You can speak to the person directly and ask for help with issues, and the person can give direct advice, which is pretty awesome. With phone calls, anything is possible, and you will be able to have much more success with it as well.

Phone calls are also good if you have a coach that is far away, or clients that are far away. Meeting for an hour or so each week does make a difference.

Skype

Skype is really the next step up in phone conversations, where you want to have a more direct conversation with the coach or client, but you also do not want to directly meet up, due to time or location constraints. With a skype call, you can either have a voice or a video chat, and the two of you can talk about whatever it is that is going on. From there, you can work out a plan of action, and then you can put it in. this gives a more personal connection, but does also require being around a computer or a device that does support this sort of action.

Coffee Shop

Now, this can be a literal coffee shop, or just a direct business location where you can meet up with your partner to discuss various elements and issues. This is a good way to directly speak about whatever it is that is going on, and from there, the two of you can work out the solution. This is great if the two of you are close enough that this is possible, and it does not always have to be a coffee shop where you do meet though does determine the quality of the session at times. Sometimes, you will want to meet up in a place where it is easy to discuss various elements with, especially if the issues are sensitive. You could meet up at the person's workplace, but do not directly meet at the office. That is never a good place to discuss the sensitive matter like this, so do not bother doing that. Instead, pick correct locations that are fitting for you.

Remember that the media you use can determine the coaching session, and it is a good rule of thumb that the closer you are to each other, the better quality the coaching session, so make sure that you keep that in mind when you are determining how to do this sort of thing. The different sort of actions that you do take will determine the future of your coaching session, and it can make all the difference in a person.

CHAPTER 5:
Questions for a Coach to Ask

Now that you know a bit about coaching, it is time to go over the important questions you should know. These questions are good for any coach to ask, and they can be used to help gain a better understanding of the client and the session.

1) May I ask you a few questions?

    This is used to help broaden the playing field, and it will help you get a better connection with the person.

    Possible answers: sure. No.

    Second question: why not?

    Action: deal with getting the question answered and any sorts of tensions related to this

2) What was great about your life this week?

    This is used to help get the client to tell you about their life. This can also be used to help you get a better understanding of their situation, and get them willing to talk.

    Possible answers: various answers about good or bad things

    Second question: what was good about that? Tell me more.

3) Have you improved yourself this week?

   This is good especially for fitness coaching, because you will be able to have them see what they've done to improve themselves and it does make a difference in people

   Possible answer: various answers as to what they did improving. Sometimes they might say they didn't improve.

   Second question: what did you want to do with those words? What do you want to continue to improve on?

4) What did you get done this week?

   This is a good question to ask to show production in an area of life, and you can eve go into detail on if that aligns with a goal or not.

   Possible answers: saying anything about what they accomplished, and the elements of it.

   Second question: how does that align with the goal you have in mind. What could be done about that?

5) Do you want to be coached on this??

   This is a good question that you can ask if you are given some sort of explanation on various elements a person accomplished.

   Possible answers: yes/no. explanation of what.

   Second question: where do you want to be coached then? How does this fit in with what you want to be coached on?

Coaching Questions

6) Did you have any struggles this week?

   This can be used to assess where someone fell short, and where you should go with the next line of coaching. You can also go over what sorts of problems a person might have because of this problem.

   Possible answers: whatever they feel they struggled with.

   Second question: well, lets' focus on those elements. What can you do to rectify the struggle?

7) Did you feel empowered this week?

   This is good especially for those with confidence issues, because often, people do not realize how much they struggle until it is too late. They start to realize where they were empowered and where they need to work on themselves, and this is good for showing them what they really need to fix.

   Possible answers: yes, no I didn't.

   Second question: tell me more about it.

   Answers: explanation

   Third question: well, how can you use this to better yourself?

8) Does your story empower or disempower you?

   This is good to use if you have a client that tells you of a story of what they did, and you can show them that it might not be the best or it might be best to speak about.

Answers: yes/no

Second question: well, how can you switch the situations so that it does empower you?

9) Do you want to be coached on that point or did you just want to share?

Sharing is good, but you want to make sure you do not deter from the subject and make sure that it is something that the person wants coaching on

Possible answers: yes/no. I wanted to share. I felt it was relevant, etc.

Second question: well, what do you want to be coached on? How does this relate to coaching?

10) Are you using your experiences and problems to grow or beat yourself up?

This can be a question that could be a hard pill to swallow, because often we use our sad experiences as a pity party more than anything else. But, if you do realize that you can grow from this, it does make all the difference, and you will be able to have a much better experience in the future.

Possible answers: I am using it to grow. I am using it as a berating tool.

Second question: how can you use what happened to grow instead of being problematic?

Coaching Questions

11) What can you do to get a better result next time?

    This is a good one to look at for those who are working to implement something into their lives. For those who are working to better themselves, this is often a tool used to see what they can do to improve it.

    Possible answers: the explanation of results and talking about what they could do better. Sometimes not realizing what they could do better.

    Second question: what were the problems you suffered from with this and how could you use what you learned here to make it better?

12) How honest have you been with this problem towards yourself and others?

    Sometimes the client is not willing to be honest with them, and that can be a problem in it of itself. It is time that you start getting them on the right track, and you can do so by talking to them and getting the truth out of the person.

    Possible answers: I haven't been super honest with it, I've been somewhat honest with it, I haven't been honest, or I have been honest.

    Possible second question: what can you do to become more honest? What will it take to be honest about the situation?

13) Can I give an observation?

    This is a very important one, and it is one you will have to be careful with. Some people love to hear observations on actions the coach sees, others, not so much. Be careful with this one in particular, because it could cause a lot more drama than you would care to have if used wrong, that's for sure.

Possible answers: sure, that's fine. No that is not okay.

Second question: alright, I will not say it/say the observation to you.

Possible answers: that makes sense/thank you for not observing.

As a note, this one is very important to get the consent of the person you are working with. For one, people often do not realize that this can be hurtful to some people, and it is not necessarily the easiest thing to get ahold of. Instead of asking right way and simply assuming, you can use this to get express consent from your client before you dive into this sort of action.

14) Is this the problem or the solution?

With many coaching sessions, sometimes people will mistake the problems for the solution, and often, it is something that does happen with time. For those that are working to figure the way around this, you should take the time to see if that is a problem, or if that is the solution. This can make a huge difference in terms of what might go down, and often, you have to look to see the problem or the solution to do something about it, so make sure that you get ahold of what it is before you continue.

Possible answers: yes this is a problem/no this is a solution.

Coaching Questions

Second question: then what is the problem/solution to this problem/solution?

15) How would you like the situation to be?

    This is especially good if you are working on a problem and have no clue how to counteract this. Sometimes envisioning the situation can be the way to help improve this sort of thing. It also works well, especially for those that are working to improve their life.

    Possible answers: working on building the situation, and then starting to envision how to do it.

    Second question: what is the plan you need to take to get to that solution?

16) What is stopping you?

    This is good for just about any sort of coaching session. For many people' look at what is stopping them, and often, this can be something that can make a big difference within many people. You have to know what the problem is, what the solution, is, and what is stopping you from getting to the solution. This can include toxic people.

    Possible answers: a list of people and things that are stopping you from reaching your goals.

    Second question: with those handled, how real would it be? What would you need to do to reach those goals?

17) Is there anyone bothering you?

Sometimes, the problem is not an object, but rather a person. Toxic people can be a nightmare, and for many, it can create quite the disturbance. However, if you within a coaching session start to realize the impact this is making, you will be able to see just who is causing problems, and what to do to create the solution to this.

Possible answers: The naming of people that are bothering you.

Second question: what can you do to bring a solution to this problem?

Possible answers: talking about the solutions to the problems at hand and going from there.

18) What does this mean to you?

If you are going over a plan, sometimes you say a lot, but you do not really get it. As a coach, you need to ask this so that the person has the express understanding on how this will work, and how you can use this to better yourself.

Possible answers: an explanation on the various means of what this means to them, a possible explanation.

Second question: how can you apply this?

You might have to go over this with someone a few times before they really get it, and it does help with the understanding of it all.

Coaching Questions

19) Are you focused on what's wrong, or what's right?

Sometimes we do not really look at the good, but only the bad. We need to make sure that we take the time to look at the good in life, and not just focus on the bad elements. In truth, this can make all the difference for some that are out there, and it does help if you are being overly judgmental about various actions.

Possible answers: various explanations on whether it is good or bad.

Second question: how can you focus more on what's right instead of wrong? What will shift your moral compass in that manner?

20) Is this the truth, or is it just hearsay?

With some clients, they might just go off of what some of the people might say, and other times, they will tell you directly what it is that is going on. You need to make sure that you do get the full story out of people, and from there, you go on and make sure that you get the full details from them.

Possible answers: this is a real thing/this was heard.

Second question: can you give me the full answers then/can you figure out the solution to the problem at hand?

21) How can you find out more information?

Sometimes, some clients do not realize that they do not know, and it is up to them to get the full details on things. With this however, you will be able to improve the mindset by making sure that you get everything squared away. You can have them search for more.

Possible answers: talk about looking for more information.

Second question: how soon can you get that information?

Possible answers: tells when they can.

Third question: what can you benefit from learning about this sort of element?

22) Do you want this for your own sake or is it for someone else?

Sometimes, some clients do things just for others, and sometimes for themselves. You need to get the full answer, and make sure they're not doing it because someone else said.

So

Possible answers: I'm doing this for myself. I'm doing this for others.

Second question: how can you work on that to do it for yourself?

23) Is this giving you energy or draining you of energy?

This is another important one, because it does determine whether a person is helpful or not. It also determines whether an action is good for you, or bad for you.

Coaching Questions

Possible answers: this is helping/not helping.

Second question: how could you turn the tables with this to make sure that it is giving you the help you need?

24) Is it really making a big difference in your life?

Sometimes, people believe that what they are doing makes all the difference, when it does not. You have to watch for this, and make sure that it is making a big impact.

Possible answers: it is/it is not.

Second question: how can you change this to help make a difference?

25) Do you know your limits?

Knowing your limits is very important, because sometimes people do not know that, and then they start to become slightly hung up on that sort of thing. You need to make sure you do not overdo it for your sake, and for the sake of others.

Possible answers: I do/do not. Describe it.

Second question: how can you become fully aware of your limits?

26) What do you consider your strengths>?

Knowing your strengths is essential to the success of your life, and it is insanely helpful as well. Knowing is half the battle, and it is what people will need do know to be successful in life.

Possible answer: list the strengths we have.

Second question: how can you use the strengths listed to better yourself and others?

27) What is the benefit to having this problem?

Sometimes problems have benefits, and with coaching, you have to be willing to explore all of that before making a true, big decision in life.

Possible answer: listing some of the benefits to this problem. Sometimes it might be not knowing.

Second question: well, what can this problem do to help you?

28) Will this problem help you or hurt you?

Sometimes though, some problems will hurt you instead of help. That is why you have to pick your battles and make sure that you are not doing something that will not work for you. Be smart, but also be wary.

Possible answers: the client says that it hurts/helps.

Second question: would you be better off if you dropped this problem? Why wouldn't you be?

29) What does your gut feeling say about this?

Sometimes, if you are at a loss for what to do, the surefire way to understand is to trust your gut. Doing that can make all the difference, that's for sure. It is simple, and it is effective.

Possible answers: I have a good/bad feeling about this sort of thing.

Second question: well, are you going to listen to your gut? Would you benefit from listening to what your gut has to say?

30) Is this problem related to something you have done before?

Sometimes connecting your problems can be something beneficial for you, and often, it can be something that will help you out. Seeing how various problems connect will do you more good than harm, because you might get to see where it would fit with everything

Possible answers: explaining how it does fit in.

Second question: what do you need to do with this current problem as it relates to the previous problem to get somewhere with it?

31) Do you have rules getting in the way of life?

Sometimes you might have some rules that you have thrown in due to family, upbringing, and the like that are getting in the way of you relieving yourself and improving your lot. You need to make sure that you do not have that just sitting in there, and you do something with it.

Possible answers: yes/no I do/do not. Sometimes listing the rules as well.

Second question: will those rules be helpful in your life if you kept them? Is it possible to do away with them?

32) How long has this been on your mind?

Knowing how long it is been on your mind does help. Sometimes, it can make all the difference and you can certainly have a much better experience with this if you do realize it is been on your mind for a while and you are working to fix it.

Possible answer: listing how long it is been on your mind.

Second question: what would you do if the problem was gone?

33) Is this similar to a problem you have experienced before?

Sometimes, seeing the connection to these problems and how similar it might be will make a difference in your life. You can use this to help you see the connections you are making, and it can help you really determine what it is that you are going for, along with the possible elements to keep in mind before you start to work on making sure that you have the problem taped.

Possible answer: yeah it is. Explanation of problem.

Second question: what can you do to use the information you gave me to solve this current problem?

34) Would you be able to change your mindset on this problem?

Sometimes you need to realize that you have got to change your minds on problems. It is important that you realize this, because it does come about sometimes.

Possible answers: I can change it/I cannot change it.

Second question: what would need to be done to change your mind on this?

35) Is this a real goal or a pipe dream?

Looking at the reality of the goal is very important. Some people do not realize this, and often, it is something that they are refusing to see for themselves. But, if you see that it is a real goal and if you realize that it might be a pipe dream in certain cases, you will be able to do something about that, and you can certainly do a lot to change it, that's for sure.

Answers: yeah it is real/yeah it might be a pipe dream.

Second question: what can you do to make this a realistic goal and not a pipe dream?

36) Does this goal coincide with your values?

You want to make sure that you are doing this for you, especially with goals at hand. Even if it is something small, you will want to make sure that you have all of that in mind and at hand, for it can make a major difference.

Possible answers: yes it does/does not coincide with my values.

Second question: how can you align the goal to let it fit with you?

37) Is this goal building you up, or is it a slog?

Sometimes you want to make sure that the goal you do have in mind is a realistic one that will work for you. You want something that inspires you, allows you to play around and make sure that you are happy, not something that is what you struggle to do with. You should make sure that the goal inspires you, not haunts you like a bad ghost.

Possible answers: it is taking a lot out of me/it helps

Second question: what can you do to not make this goal such a slog?

These coaching questions can help you as a coach inspire others, and it can be used to improve the worth of the person now, and into the future.

CHAPTER 6:
Questions for a Person to Know

Now that you know of questions that can be used for a coach, these can be used personally to benefit yourself and improve what you know. This is great to help a coach think critically on all coaching sessions to improve this.

1) What did you accomplish this week?

    This is good to show a coach just what they did this week, what they can use to help benefit their lives for themselves and how to improve on that.

    Possible answer: the various people they helped, or maybe they didn't help.

    Second question: what can you do to help more this week? How can you use what you have done to help yourself?

2) Who did you serve?

    This is a good gauge for those who are looking to see who they helped this week, and also looking to assist those that are looking to understand the scope of how they helped.

    Possible answers: naming various people that they helped and how it fits in.

    Second question: to what extent did you help these people? How did your help benefit them?

This will help the coach really understand to what extent they are helping this person.

3) How did you grow this week as a coach?

This is a good question to ask any coach, coaching is not just something that you do with another person, but rather, it is something that you need to remember to grow in as well.

Possible answers: various situations where the coach was able to grow in different ways with their coaching.

Second question: how much of an impact did this have on you personally?

4) Is there anything you would like to improve on yourself?

As a coach, you have to learn that you need to improve too. It is not just a one-way street. You can always work on various coaching means, and from there, you can definitely make a better and bigger difference as a coach in it of yourself.

Possible answers: various information and traits that you want to improve for whatever reason.

Second question: how would improving this help in your ability as a coach? What sort of impact would this make on your clients?

Coaching Questions

5) Are you a strong enough leader for yourself and your clients?

This is good to look at, because sometimes as coaches, it can be hard to realize the impact that you make on yourself. You need to realize that over time, you will need to improve on your ability to be a leader, because a good leader will empower others.

Answer: yes/no

Second question: what can you do to improve on that?

Possible answers: various traits to work on.

Third question: what sort of plan of action can you implement to better yourself?

6) Do you feel like you are helping others?

This is a good question to pique interest with. The reason why you do this is because often, people do not realize they need to be happy when it comes to helping, which is why people need to remember that it is also based on them whether or not they are being helped.

Answers: yes/no

Second question: what can you do to further help others? What do you feel you are doing wrong in terms of assisting other people?

7) Who else will benefit?

This is a good one to ask, because sometimes people do not realize who else might benefit from this actions, and this can be a good way to get a coach to further expand themselves and give others their services.

Possible answers: my friends/family

Second question: how can you get these people to work with you and benefit from the actions you take?

8) What are you grateful for?

   We take life for granted. Plain and simple. But, if you take the time to look at yourself and see what exactly you are grateful for, you will benefit from this. It is something that can certainly help others, that's for sure.

   Possible answers: my family, friends, animals, etc.

   Second question: how can you show better gratitude for these people?

9) Who's grateful for you?

   Sometimes, we do not realize the impact that we create on others, but, with this question, you can look upon yourself and see the sort of impact you are working to improve yourself. This is a good way to help make it better for you to see just what you are doing for another person, and overall, it is a simple effective way to improve your life.

   Possible answers: listing various people who are grateful for you.

   Second question: how do you know they are grateful for you?

   Possible answers: say why they show it.

Third question: what can you do better to improve this?

10) Are you happy?

    Being happy is something we do not really realize we're not feeling until it is too late. Sometimes we have to see that we're not creating the happiness we should be, and often, it is something that can be shocking for everyone.

    Possible answers: yes/no I'm happy/not happy.

    Second question: what is causing you unhappiness?

    Possible answers: people/situations.

    Third question: what can you do to take control of the situation?

11) Are you honest with yourself?

    Being honest with yourself is something that many coaches do not realize they forget to do. You have to be honest to really be successful. Sometimes, if you are lying to yourself, it comes off obviously in a coaching session, and from there, it can become a major problem.

    Possible answers: yes/no I'm being honest/not honest.

    Second question: what is preventing you from being honest to yourself?

    Possible answers; people/places that are preventing honesty.

    Third question: how can you prevent this from becoming a problem?

12) Do you believe your coaching works?

   You have to know and feel that your coaching works to make sure that you are doing the right thing. It is understandable when it seems you are not doing well with your coaching, and thereby do take some time and effort to make sure that you work on that as well. If your coaching works, you will work, and over time, it does make a difference.

   Possible answers: yes/no I do/do not.

   Second question: what is stopping you from feeling like you can make this work?

13) Do you have a goal with every client?

   Having a goal with your clients will keep you inspired to do better, and often, it can be something that will really help you. You want to have goals, because it will allow you to fulfill them over time and give yourself and others the life they deserve.

   Answer: yes/no I have that.

   Second question: what kinds of goals can you set up with your clients to ensure that you have one?

14) Will your choices with the clients bring you forward or not?

   You have to make sure that the choices you make with them benefit not only them, but you as well. Making the correct decisions does play a major role in improving the coaching between a client and his coach.

Coaching Questions

Possible answers: yes it does. No it is not as much

Second question? What can you do to improve that and bring you forward along with them?

15) Will the advice you give bring better benefits to others

You want to make sure that you are using this to help benefit others. If you feel that it is not helping them, then you need to look at yourself and strive to change just that. You need to make sure you are giving those help and advice, not problems and such.

Possible answers: it is helping them. It is not helping them.

Second question: what can you do to bring better benefits to others?

16) How does that solution help a client?

You want to make sure that the solutions you present to them will help your client in multiple ways. Figuring out the best means to help your client and the solutions you give will in turn allow you to have a much better, healthier mans to improving the life that you are working to have with others.

Possible answers: it helps in various ways. Say how it does.

Second question: what can you do to further help a client with this solution?

17) Is there any advice you would wish to get out of your system before you spread it to other clients?

Knowing what works and what does not work, and having the decency not to spread it to other clients, is a major part of coaching. For those that are working to coach, the best thing to do is to make sure that you give only good advice, because these people do rely on you, and they want the benefits listed.

Possible answers: various sort of beliefs that you have.

Second question: what can you do to get rid of them? Can you get rid of them now?

You should work with this in mind and start to work on getting rid of the possible bad things that might be lurking about.

18) What's the worst that can happen with that advice?

You might have some advice that you are trying to determine if it is good or bad for the client. This is important, because often, people think the advice is awful, but they do need to look at whether or not a person can benefit from this, and what you can do to improve this sort of thing.

Possible answers: list out the problems with it.

Second question: based off that, is the advice worth it to use, or not to use?

Coaching Questions

19) Is there a downside to the dreams you have

You might have a dream as a coach to get your client somewhere, but you also need to make sure that it works for you. Being smart and knowing whether or not some advice will work or not work is essential, and it is very important.

Possible answers: list the downsides to his, if any.

Second question: is there a way to continue with the pathway while limiting the downsides of this?

20) What is stopping you from giving advice to that client?

Sometimes there are a few things that are stopping you from really giving the best advice that you can to the client. You might have your own personal dislikes, or whatever you so choose. You should make sure that you know what is stopping you, and what exactly is going rough your mind, to rally see what you can do to benefit this.

Possible answers: talk about what is stopping you.

Second question: what sort of actions can you do to prevent the stops from getting in the way?

21) Who wouldn't like it if you did the right thing?

Some people out there hate the concept of people being smart and logical. They hate when people are doing the right thing and benefitting, and especially as coaches, there is a sort of need to sometimes withhold information. However, sometimes you need to make sure that you choose the right actions, so what you believe is best, and know who would or wouldn't like it.

Possible answers: listing of various people who might or might not like it.

Second question: is there a way to avoid these sorts of people so you do not have to worry about that?

22) Do you have to sacrifice anything to help others?

As a coach, there are moments when you work hard, and you practically sacrifice it all to be successful. However, it shouldn't just be a singular effort, and you shouldn't sacrifice too much to help others. If you are stressed out, overworked, or the like, sometimes it can be caused by not really working out how to reduce the sacrifices and such. That is why you need to realize the sacrifices, and then go from there.

Possible answers: listing the sacrifices that would need to be made if that sort of action happened.

Second question: is there a way to limit the sacrifices to answer your own personal happiness?

23) Will a new skill add to your value?

Sometimes you have to make sure that you choose the right skills. Choose skills that will add to the value, of the person, and you want to make sure that these skills the coach has for the client do add to the value. Make sure that you choose the right ones, and from there, determine what to do next.

Possible answers. It does help or does not help with it.

Coaching Questions

Second question what can I do as a coach to improve the skill in the person? What sort of skill can I substitute out to make it better for the client in question?

With coaching, you sometimes have to ask yourself the personal questions that are important about this, and you will want to ensure that you do have the right sort of question there for the person at hand. Be smart about this, make the correct decisions, and from there you will have much more success and happiness, that I'm sure of.

CHAPTER 7:
Client Coaching Questions to Ask

Now that you know a little on the coaching side, let's go over what the client needs to take from this. Often, a client can get a number of benefits out of this, and for some, this can indeed make all the difference in the world. This chapter will go over 21 questions the client should ask.

1) Is this advice going to help me?

   You want to make sure that this advice will help with the problem at hand. Often, some coaches who are starting out might pull you in a different direction, and sometimes, a client is bad with explaining. You should ask the coach what sort of ways this will benefit you as well.

   Possible answer: the coach's response in terms of the actions you must take.

   Second question: how will this help me improve my skills?

2) What can I benefit from learning this advice?

   You want to make sure that as a client you are getting the best advice possible. With coaching, sometimes it is hard to explain what you really want, and with this, you will be able to make sure that you get exactly what you need, and you can benefit from this.

   Possible answers: the coach explains the benefits of learning this.

Coaching Questions

Second question/plan: take it all into consideration and then start to plan accordingly.

3) Do you feel I need to hone my skills?

   Sometimes, you might need to ask the coach if it is necessary to hone your personal skills. You can make sure that you have a good relationship with the coach by finding out what sort of skills you will want to take, the skills you believe are right, and from there, you can move forward and work on the right skills for you.

   Possible answer: the coach tells you a bit about the skills.

   Second question: what actions do I need to take to improve this?

4) What kind of plan of action should I be taken?

   Sometimes the coach can give you a good plan of action to move forward. You can use this to help benefit not only your life, but the life of others too. This is especially important if you are running into this sort of problem, and often, it can really make a difference in your life. You should always have a plan of action before you begin.

   Possible answers: the coach gives you a sort of plan.

   Second question: what is the first step needed to get started with this plan?

5) How can I take my strengths and put them forward?

You want to know what your strengths are, so you can push them forward. But often, people do not know what to do about this sort of thing initially, and often, they might need help discovering their strengths and using it. You should, as a client, as your coach for help in this.

Possible answers: an explanation of the strengths at hand and then pushing them forward as well.

Second question: is there a plan to push my strengths to the forefront?

6) How do I limit my weaknesses?

Many times, the client might be knowledgeable of the weaknesses, and often, they might start to think that it is smart to look at limiting it. However, they might not know how. A good question to ask the coach is how you can limit the weaknesses of things, and what you can do to make sure that you get that fixed up.

Possible answers: an explanation of weaknesses.

Second question: what is the first step to take when it comes to limiting my weakness?

7) What sort of changes can I make with what I have?

You need to know as a client what sort of changes to make with the life that you have and everything that you have got. With this though, you can do so easily, and without too much of a hassle. A coach can often tell you exactly where you need to go with this, and it does make a big different.

Possible answers: coach explains the changes that need to be made

Second question: where do my skills line up with this?

8) How do I increase my resources?

   As a client, you will need to know how to increase the resources that you have, and often, it is something that you will have to face with time. You do want to make sure that you have a good idea of the resources you have got, because it does make a big difference in your life.

   Possible answers: assessing all resources and figuring out an answer.

   Second question: where do I begin with increasing the value of my resources?

9) Am I just following a pipe dream or is this realistic?

   As a client, you have to control the reality of your dream as well. With a coach, you might sometimes get the answer that it is a pipe dream, and from there you will need to increase the plan of action and go for what needs to be fixed up. With this question, you will be able to ask your coach in a realistic way if you are on the right track, of if it is really intelligent to follow through with this sort of thing. When you do get the answer to that, do not fret, but instead realize that often, we might be following dreams that aren't necessarily the smartest to face.

10) What sort of advice can you give me on (insert problem here)?

As a client, you might think you have it relatively figured out, but the coach is another person, a guy with different experiences, and it can be almost essential to ask the other person for help from time to time. By asking your client if you can get advice from them, you can then move forward, using the advice that you do have to make sure that you are going the right way, moving against the right pathway. Doing this will help you, and over time, it will make a big difference in your life. Try it, because in truth, this sort of advice is the type you never know what you might get, and it might make all the difference.

11) Will I be able to overcome my fears?

As a client, you might have a ton of fears, and often, it is something that is scary to think about, but over time, you will start to realize that it is possible to overcome the fears that you have. Fear is a matter of lie itself, and over time, you will start to realize that you will indeed get there over time. Overcoming fears are something that you will need to make sure that you get ahold of, and you will want to feel the urge to overcome them. A coach will improve the life that you are living, and you should make sure that you are smart about how this goes, and over time, you will achieve great success.

12) How can I improve on this situation to give it value

A coach has kind of a bird's eye view on the situation at hand, and it can be remarkably helpful. By looking at the situation and improving on it so that you can be valuable, you will be able to see the truth everything. With this, you will start to see it all, and over time, it will create quite the impact, and in turn, it will vastly improve your lot, and your worth as well. By asking your coach how to improve this and create a valuable asset out of this, you will have much more success, and in turn much more happiness.

13) Am I acting on logic of impulse

Sometimes, a client does not realize how they are acting until it is too late. If you realize that you are indeed acting out of impulse instead of acting out of logical, you will be able to see the difference in it. As a client, the coach will be able to guide you in the right direction, and if they say you are indeed acting out of impulse versus logic, you should ask how to prevent this, how you as a client can improve on this sort of action now, and into the future. A coach is there to lead you on the right pathway, and over time, this can be used to help you stay in your lane and get yourself fully on the right pathway to success.

14) How do I go about talking to empower and help others?

You shouldn't be just getting help from the coach in empowering, but you should use it to empower others. With coaching, a client should always learn to empower other people. By asking your coach how they do it, getting the full understanding of what I is that they do, and understanding it, you will be able to achieve great success, better understanding, and much more fun in life. Remember, as a coach, they are working to build you up, so it is only fair that you work to empower other people as well.

15) How do I increase my courage to change my life?

A scary thing about being a client is the fact that you might change. Sometimes, you might worry about changing your life for the better, but you do want to figure out how to increase the courage that you need to do this. Yes, this does take courage and yes, you are going to need to be brave. But true bravery is realizing that this indeed does exist, and you need to be realistic as well that the smart thing to do is to make sure that you do the right thing. Do make sure that the courage you have does increase, and over time, you will have much more success.

16) What sort of schedule should I have on this?

For a client, the best thing to know is the layout of their day and the schedule which will work. Taking on this big of an endeavor is quite adventurous, and over time, it surely does become something that you need to face. However, if you figure out a schedule and formulate it to success, you will be able to improve the way things are. Over time, it'll get better, you just need to make sure that you do have the right mindset with this. Having an adequate and smart schedule is the way to success, and you should consult the coach to ensure you do the right thing.

17) Is this really a need or value for myself?

With advice, you want to make sure that it is valuable. While a coach might think it is, and they might tell you something about it, you need to make sure that it works for you. Over time it will become obvious that you do need to watch for the correct sort of reasons that you do make sure to do this sort of thing. You want to make sure that value is there, and it is placed on the coaching session. With this as well, you will be able to have much more success and happiness, and you will do so without any sorts of failure or problems.

18) Have you faced a problem like this before?

A coach might have the experience needed to face this problem. Shocking, right? It shouldn't be. Coaches are people like you and me, and you want to make sure that it is smart to talk about this problem and you have a good grip on this. Talking to the coach and asking for their advice and input on this is something that many people struggle with, because often, coaches might seem like these big, scary guys that you do not talk to about these sorts of thing. But being smart, making sure that you can trust them, can give you the information you need to face the problems you have.

19) What sort of experience would I need to overcome this problem?

You would need to make sure that you have the right sort of experiences on hand to improve this sort of thing. With coaching, you do want to make sure that you get a coach who can tell you of the experiences and skills that you will need to generate success with this. A common problem with some people who go into coaching, is they believe that talking to the coach about such experience is wrong in some sort of fashion. But it is not always that way, and you will want to make sure you are comfortable as well with the experiences that you have. Get experience to overcome the problem, and from there, you will feel much better and be better off.

20) What's the impact I'll create with this?

You will want to know the impact you can create with this, because often, it does determine what sort of reaction you will get out of this. Knowing the impact of your actions and what this will create is essential to success, and over time, it does improve the effects of this. Knowing what the future will hold will allow you to formulate a plan of action to truly benefit from this, and you will feel so much better over time as a result of these endeavors.

21) How can I accomplish more with less of the effort put forward?

Accomplishing more with not as much effort and becoming efficient is the name of the game with this. As a client, you will want to ensure that you do take into consideration what you are going through, and you will want to improve the nature of this. You will want to ask your coach about how to become more efficient. They can lead you in the right direction, improve your success, and in general create happiness. Doing this does make a difference, and it will continue to do so no matter what.

With coaching, you have to get the client's perspective as well, and you will want to make sure that you do so before you continue. The client should be open to asking questions, and from there it can determine what should be done next, the actions needed to be taken, and the next step to achieve the success of or both parties.

CHAPTER 8:
Questions for the Client to Ask Themselves

Now that we have gone over what clients should ask coaches, now it is time to go over what a client should ask himself or herself. This is important, because it makes a difference, and with these 20 questions, you will know exactly what you should ask before things get out of hand.

1) What am I pretending not to know?

    Sometimes, some clients will leave their life in a state of not-knowing. They might start to pretend that they do not know the answer to the solution, but that certainly is not the case. Instead of deluding yourself and pretending that you do not know anything, start to work on improving yourself by seeing that there is some things you do know, but you are pretending not to know. Knowing this, you will have a much better experience in your life, and one that is much better for you as well.

2) Am I acting out of the faith I have, or fear?

    Sometimes, some of us do act and react to situations out of fear. You have to know this, and often, it can be scary to see. You should know the difference between the two of them, and over time, it does become easier as you ask yourself that. Do make sure that you work with yourself, see the difference in that, and work towards fixing that up. Often, making sure you know the difference between the two can make all the difference in the future of your life and what you are trying to make it become.

3) If I wasn't scared, what would I do?

Sometimes, the reason why we do not act the way we went to is out of sheer fear. It is obvious when it happens, and in truth, it is hard to face. But you have to realize that the only thing to fear is fear itself, and often, if we aren't scared of something, we will accomplish it. As a client, you need to realize that the reason why you are not reaching for the stars is the fear of the unknown. Once you see that, you can start to plan your life accordingly, and through this, have much more success as well.

4) How do I increase my sureness in myself?

Increasing the sureness in yourself is something that you will have to do. You will want to look at yourself, see what you are doing to either improve or not improve your lot, and from there, start to look at how sure you are. You need to question how you can be sure in yourself, because often, the reason why people aren't confident is because of how unsure they are. By making sure that you are sure of things, you will be able to increase the success you are working towards, and you will feel way more confident in your decisions.

5) Am I confident in my decisions?

Also with that, is confidence in your decisions? Have you ever decided on something, and then you immediately regretted it? Yeah, that's something that can often come about as a result of not being confident in your life choices. However, if you start to question whether you are, it brings you forward, and this is something you will need to ask yourself. It could present another problem you can work with the coach to solve, or it will just simply bring to light all of the problems at hand. If you are confident, you can do whatever it is that you need to do, and from there, you will have much more success as well.

6) If my life was around my values how would it be like?

Sometimes visioning this and seeing what it would be like can make a huge impact on yourself. Seeing the extent that it does take and the way your life would change can help you see which values are good, and which ones aren't so good. However, you can also get the rude awakening that you do seem to get at times, which might show that you do not have the best values. This is really one of the best exercises to see your place and the values you have, and over time, you can work to improve that, make it much better, and in general, improve everything in some way, shape or form.

7) If I could take one step to make a difference, what would it be?

Sometimes seeing how you can make an impact with just one step can change things. With life, the little things do go a long way, but we take them for granted. We certainly do, and it is something we are not willing to admit to ourselves until its too late. But taking the time to pick up the little seeds we've planted, seeing them for what they are, and doing something about it, can change the game in general. Instead of just holding onto the idea that you cannot change things, start to look upon yourself and see exactly how to do it. Do not be afraid of what the others might say, but instead, work to make the impact you know you can.

8) What will I accomplish today to make a difference?

This is a way to really look at the life you have to offer, and from there, start to determine what you can do to make an impact in the world. This is a great thing to ask yourself when you wake up first thing in the morning and are planning your day. Working to at least accomplish something every single day can make a huge difference, and over time, it will certainly improve your understanding of things as well. You owe it to yourself to do this, and it will help you on many different fronts.

9) Will this advice help or hinder me?

As a client, you might get advice from those outside of the circle of where you get advice from, and you might start to question it. This is a good piece of advice for those sorts of clients who hear a lot of hearsay from their friends and peers, and they do not know what to do with it. This is especially good if you are getting advice from a source that you are not sure whether is good or bad. Look at the advice, see it for what it is, and then determine over time if it is a good thing to have or a bad thing, and you will from there be able to do with this information what you feel is best.

10) How do I meet the needs that I have?

Sometimes, looking to see that you have needs and working to meet them can make a difference in the way you function. You should look at the needs you possess every so often, and from there, start to work on trying to improve your need for them. Sometimes, these needs will pop out at you. Other times, they will show themselves suddenly. Keep track of your needs, and from there work on trying to put it together. This is something you can ask yourselves or your coach the next time you are in a session, and they can help accordingly to steer you in the right direction and give you what you need as well.

11) What is the emotional cost of this decision?

When you are making a decision, this is in general the thing you ask yourself. With emotions, there is a cost involved. It is not a monetary cost, but in some cases it might as well be. Certain decisions have a significant emotional impact on you. You might feel good about it, you might feel bad, but you will need to remember that certain types of decisions will make an impact on you physically and emotionally, so be chary when making decisions. You should always go for the ones that create a good impact on you and your body, but also look for the decision that will not cause you so much emotional turmoil that you will not be able to function. This is an important question, and it should be asked before every major decision is made in a client's life.

12) Am I procrastinating on this decision?

Procrastination is not the key to success. It is not, and often, it can be detrimental in certain factors. Procrastination can cause you to make foolhardy decisions, so it is not the best thing in the world to do. As a client, you must ask yourself if you are procrastinating, and why you are. The answers there can open you up to new problems and such that you might want to go over with the coach. This is a great question to ask if you are worried about where you should go next, and if you are freaking over a decision. Do not procrastinate, but instead do something about this to help yourself, and to help others.

13) What am I delaying my actions?

You should also look at what you are delaying with the actions that you take. Some people subconsciously do delay personal actions because of their desire to make sure that they aren't offending people or hurting some sort of future decision. Do not hold yourself back from making correct decisions, and instead, try to look at if you are delaying the inevitable. Sometimes, if you do look at that, you will start to realize that you are delaying something, and you will see it for what it is, and then work to handle it. As you may already know in many cases, the client will refuse to jump and make plunges without their coach around, and that can create a giant impact in the future. But do not be afraid of it; instead realize what it is, and then go from there.

14) How can I learn from this problem?

As a client, you will need to learn from your mistakes. See for yourself that you have problems, and instead of trying to avoid them, face them. If you do not face them, and instead work to avoid them, you will not get anywhere. Chances are, that's probably how you got into the situation that you are in. Instead of holding back though and not learning about this, you should instead take the problem, harness it, and from there, work on improving the solution over time. It is important to know that, and you will definitely benefit from learning about where your problems go and the impact that they have in life, that is for sure. Take the time to learn, and you will certainly improve the problems and the state of them over time with that and that alone.

15) How can I enjoy learning how to solve problems?

Problems are not always things you enjoy solving. Often, you might not know how to really effectively do this sort of thing. Learning how to solve them and enjoying how to solve them will improve the way you feel about problems. Often, the reason why people hate problems it is not because problems exist, it is the fact that they have to solve them. But what if you learned how to. Maybe you can answer that for yourself, and then work on a plan to understand how to enjoy the concept of solving problems. Learning to love them is not something weird to do, but if you think about it with the fact that learning to love problems is a good thing, you will start to see the impact problems have. It is a known fact that if you do not let a problem affect you, chances are you will have a better control over the situation, and much more success to boot.

16) Is there any benefit I know of to solving these problems?

Some might not realize the benefit to solving problems. Solving problems can be your best friend though. Often, when you are against solving problems, chances are you might start to feel the problems collapse in on you and make things harder on yourself as well. However, there is quite a benefit to solving the various problems you suffer from. The fewer problems you have, the happier you will be, because often, if you take control and solve the issues at hand, you will be able to move further with this and take on new and bigger problems. That is the benefit of resolving them, and it is why people take them in. if you are working to improve yourself, the best thing for you to do is to start looking at how to solve these problems, and you will start to see the benefits come up like a flash over time, making things even better for you as well.

17) Am I working to take action of working on blind hope?

Blind hope is something that people start to push themselves into, and often, it is a big problem for some. Blind hope is how many get in trouble, and it is how clients start to falter. Often, working with blind hope is not a smart manner, and you might be lying to yourself. You need to take action, and not just rely on hope.

This can be a hard question to swallow for many people, and often, it is not easy to face. However, if you start to see that blind hope is something possible, you will be able to improve this over time, and you will stop relying on this. Stop decisions that rely on blind hope, and start to use logic to create a better, more successful situation.

18) What am I responsible?

Responsibility is something that everyone needs to face. Sometimes, a client might not realize just how much they're responsible for, and often, that can lead to a boatload of problems. Many times, the reason why people claim that they're not doing something or working on a sector of the company, is because they're not responsible. But, if you do not take responsibility, you will not be able to be successful with that area, and it can make a difference between happiness and success, and stress and displeasure in a person. Realize that your success lies in your responsibility and the ability to take on certain factors, and start to work on that to improve your life business, or the like. Doing that can make a difference, and doing so can help you in multiple ways.

19) How can I increase the zone of my responsibility?

Increasing your responsibility is something that you are going to have to do. If you are looking for increasing this, you will start to see for yourself that you are in charge of certain elements as well. By making sure that you know what you are in charge of, you can take control of it. Maybe though, after you have controlled that, you want to see how much more of this you can control. That's where the zone of responsibility comes in. You need to know what it is, where you need to be, and all the elements of it. Once you know that, you can increase, and it'll make your life all the more easier.

20) Am I working on this logically, or with my heart?

Finally, with decisions in coaching yourself, you have to look to see if you are following your head, or your heart. Your heart might tell you some gut instincts, but your head is where the correct decisions come in. do not make bad decisions, and instead, start to work with yourself. If you do start to think logically, understanding the situations and all of that, you will notice when you are working toward improving yourself, or if you are just working on blind faith.

Making sure that you follow your head with serious plans of action instead of your heart is imperative, and often, it can make all the difference with you in the future.

With coaching, it is a personal situation that you will need to take on as well. Often, working to improve yourself and taking a personal look at who you are can make everything all the better. In truth, it can be scary to have all of that, but over time, it can be something that you will start to see over time. by doing this, you will notice that it is only going to get better from here, and it can make your life so much better, easier, and more fulfilling for you as well. So do take the time to coach yourself, for it can be the best decision that you have made, because you are looking inward to yourself and seeing everything that would need to be changed over time.

CONCLUSION

Thank you again for taking the time to check out this book!

I hope you learned a lot about coaching. Coaching is a great tool to be used in really just about any situation. There are tons of uses for this, and in truth, it can be one of the best things you can do for yourself. With coaching, you will be able to take control of the situation, and over time, you will be able to do what you feel is best for the situation, and you will be able to increase the ability and drive to become better at this as well.

With that being said, it is time to talk about the next step to take. There are really two next steps for you as well, and there are two options to go. The first, is for coaches. Your next step is to take the material in the coaching section and begin to use this to help better others. It is simple, effective, and very much helpful as well. You will be able to assist your clients with reaching their goals and dreams and you can do so without too much trouble as well.

For those that are clients reading this book, your next step is to take the questions in the client section, and either start to ask your coach about them, or ask yourself. You owe it to yourself to have success, and with these questions, you will be able to have that and so much more, easily and without too much of a hassle. Do it, and you will be reaching for the stars and achieving success in no time.

BOOK RECOMMENDATION

Leadership Coaching

101 Strategies for the Coach and the Coaching Client to Becoming a True Leader

By Randy Wayne

AVAILABLE ON AMAZON.COM

JULY 2016

Made in the USA
Columbia, SC
29 November 2024

47863517R00043